# The Edge of Winter

Also by Connie Barber
*Budgerigah Flying* (1989)
*Enter Your House with Care* (1996)
*Sand* (2002)
*Between Headlands* (2006)

Connie Barber

# The Edge of Winter

## Acknowledgements

Poems in this collection have previously been published in
*Antipodes* (USA), *Australian Poetry Journal*, *Blue Dog*, *Blue
Giraffe*, *Canberra Times*, *Five Bells*, *4W*, *Malahat Review* (Canada),
*Notata*, *Poetrix*, *Poetry Monash*, *Positive Words*, *Prospect*, *Southerly*,
*Dodecahedron* (Poets Union Anthology 2010), *Metabolism*
(Australian Poetry Ltd Members Anthology 2012), *Once Upon a
Sonnet: Sonnets by today's poets* (Melbourne Shakespeare Society,
2014), *Poems 2013* (Australian Poetry Ltd Members' Anthology
2013), *Prismatics* (Poets Union Anthology 2008), *Time with the Sky*
(Newcastle Poetry Prize Anthology 2010).

\*

I thank all the friends who have shared their interest and skills in
developing these poems, particularly Ron Pretty, Judith Rodriguez,
Alex Skovron, Chris Wallace-Crabbe, and the Thursday writing
group – Charles D'Anastasi, Paul Dolphin, Christina McCallum,
Gita Mammen and Barbara Orlowska.

*The Edge of Winter*
ISBN 978 1 74027 995 6
Copyright © Connie Barber 2015
Cover painting by the author

First published 2015 by
**GINNINDERRA PRESS**
PO Box 3461 Port Adelaide 5015 Australia
www.ginninderrapress.com.au

# Contents

| | |
|---|---|
| **In Their Own Time** | **7** |
| The Child on the Cliff | 9 |
| Friend Crow | 10 |
| Exchange | 11 |
| Hanging On | 12 |
| Unencumbered Age | 13 |
| The Lasting Touch | 15 |
| In Their Own Time | 16 |
| I Want to Write a Poem | 17 |
| To the Sea | 18 |
| Winter Fog | 19 |
| Cliffs of Fall | 20 |
| Second Thoughts | 21 |
| Portrait of a Poem | 22 |
| Fantasy | 23 |
| In the Time | 24 |
| Traveller | 25 |
| Tree Peony | 26 |
| The Long Drought | 27 |
| Duck Business on Grey Goose Creek | 28 |
| **Time on the Merri Merri Creek** | **31** |
| Ninety Soon Enough | 33 |
| Time on the Merri Merri Creek | 34 |
| The Country of Nothing | 38 |
| Duck Circles | 39 |
| Mistake | 40 |
| After Drought a Day of Wind | 42 |
| Reply | 43 |
| The Colour of Water | 44 |

| | |
|---|---|
| Welcome to This Space | 45 |
| Sudden Rain | 46 |
| The Creek's Summer | 47 |

## The Edge of Winter — 49

| | |
|---|---|
| Having a Good Day | 51 |
| All the Paths Are Dry | 52 |
| The End of Winter | 53 |
| Continuance | 54 |
| Transition | 55 |
| The Portuguese Fish Basket | 56 |
| Holiday | 59 |
| Pool | 60 |
| The Table | 61 |

## The Dark Side of the Eclipse — 63

| | |
|---|---|
| No Longer | 65 |
| Edge | 66 |
| Return | 68 |
| Inside Out | 69 |
| Fig Reply | 70 |
| The House I Have Left Behind | 71 |
| Still Life – A Portrait | 72 |
| The Large Hadron Collider | 73 |
| There is a Time of Day | 74 |
| The Dark Side of the Eclipse | 75 |
| The Poem I Will Forget | 76 |
| The Creek in Winter | 77 |

# In Their Own Time

# The Child on the Cliff

(1926)

The child on the cliff looked down
on flowering peach trees trembling
in the sun. Bees busy visiting
crimson hearts, close enough to hear
but not to touch.

Below the cliff she climbed
rough bark, dark with age, thick
trunks, twisted limbs shaking
in the wind below a blinding light's
black stars, a shivering roof.

Terrified she slid across sharp bark,
grazed and bleeding stood
under a convulsed forest.
A black snake slid across
the ground. Bamboos clacked,
shaking in the wind.

Too young to know the secret
underbelly of the print of beauty,
hope and love, she ran, old enough
to sense how terror grew
in sun and wind and flowered.

## Friend Crow

I sit on a reaped hill.
Grass withers before drought.
On the post by the wire gate
stands friend crow: the white-eyed raven.

He calls, rises on fingered wings.
Glossy as a peacock, he shines
like a rainbow, keeps the bounds
of his territory, living within desolation.

# Exchange

Clown silence speaks dumb pain.
I should laugh, words are a joke.
Approval mocked conversation
that cannot get off to a good start.

Any moment emotion might break
into enthusiasm and the world crumble.
I drop attempts to guess or second-guess
where speech might lead.

I'd heard the wrong word or said
something incomprehensible too often.
Unspoken words hover. The child
dialogue died years ago;

its spirit haunts morning,
a correct ghost knows its place.
I dodge around it,
joke with it from behind,

hear backwards but
shout lines onto the page
without emotion of course.

# Hanging On

You cling to the known edge
In limitless fog. Swing
Hand over hand in thick air,
Raw, quickening, blind,
Over a swelling tide
Through known boundaries.

On an ordinary day fog clears.
Shadows cut sharp as knives.

Ordinary night offers no protection
From flaying light. Here you are found
Brilliant in clear dark.

# Unencumbered Age

This could be the quiet time, the serenity
of age, self-satisfied and whole.
There is the changing city, unfamiliar freeways,
responsibility ending at the front gate,
some friendship, some respect perhaps,
contempt – you can't deny the young
their narrow eyes. The time of peace.
But there are those sneaky genes. Their trace
won't sit passively.

How old was Socrates? Not very, by my count.
Seventy, the prime of age, the artist at the height
of power as in a favourable review,
but this time true.

You meet the first school-time thrill,
shaking with Alzheimer, hear of the lover
his heart stopping in another country, see
the great achiever fading to inevitable
nothing, and the warrior, oaths
forgotten, shrinking to
faltering immobility.

The school rival, cells cringing into overgrowth,
the beauty, boneless, bent like a safety pin,
the athlete fracturing anything
at the drop of a tea-towel,
all keeping on and up.

The bones of elders who might be the epitome
of quiet and reflection stick out like plucked
chooks' wings. The choice of each day's clothes
barely worth the challenge. But they come, the days,
and go, not counted, scarcely bound into a consummation,
a memorial worth living for.

Then there is the last innings of the flawed,
forgotten in the care of strangers hardly knowing
what and which and where now is, the future
too caught up in front windows,
the revolutions ahead.

One or two of the silent drop out
quietly. You watch and wonder
when will the final game begin.
It has already.

# The Lasting Touch

Hands warm and dry, still muddy from the game.
A delicate touch that did not last, the lightning touch.

The shoulder in the car touching when it need not,
warmth to hold or withdraw, a magnet of need.

Eyes golden brown, remembering war we both knew,
seeing more than clear day, no brooding.

Holding eyes, still and dark, looking
from the photograph's closed locket

long after it should be gone. The name conjured
in the night. The wrong name. The touch that failed.

The death, heard on the radio. How many
years – there – here – a name barely held.

A newsreader recalls the voice, the touch
too long ago to have still been remembered

here echoed in hands muddied after planting, weeding,
pruning, washed clean, a touch to forget to forget.

# In Their Own Time

I

A strong south-westerly behind the ebb
angers water to rise roaring, sucking
as though it were the flood, strong and cold,
the disruption of opposition:

water and wind, the moon, its gravity
and the spinning globe, like confronting bulls;
wind, torn from its cyclonic heart's
loss of order into a disoriented bearing.

Water roars like wind, flies as clotted air –
condensed violence only turning time
can mediate to song between tides,
or turn quiet withdrawal into fierce duality.

II

Today the northerly lies gently on the flow.
Water is talking to the rocks, whispering
to the opposing wind in counterpoint
with its slow drumbeat on the sand.

# I Want to Write a Poem

I would write a poem. Can you know
my lack? Perhaps you do. I do not need
your ridicule or courtesy. I have heard
of lovers younger called that mocking
slangy gibe – I am the younger fool,
a failed incompetent in wisdom's school,

lacking practice, how to play the game,
the rules unknown, and you are there,
an echo, daily close, intangible.

I want to hear your voice. I want to feel
your touch. I want to write a love poem
when all the clocks have slowed and time is swift,
pretending contact's only in the mind
knowing you'd never choose to be unkind.

# To the Sea

Here I am, a gene's accident
praising the sea for its quiet times,
its wild days and fierce nights,
its acceptance and its danger.

I walked this littoral curing a broken foot,
swam with a carved-up shoulder,
swam and walked, walked and swam
in all moods, and it has, with
accidental people, given me back
hands and feet, arms and legs.

Today under wind from the east the sea
is welcoming. Its lowest withdrawal, pulsing
like a heart renewing life, sings
an irregular tune, a syncopated beat,
never the same note or word or rhythm.
This mercurial sea bears wind and storm,
its spinning currents hold together
all god's accidents.

I can leave the uncertain surface
to touch the dappled floor, seagrass,
seaweed, sand, the edge of dark,
the shadow of power that cuts chasms,
that builds mountains,
that flings it all to foam.

# Winter Fog

The bay without arms, without limit. Sea-fog
has closed the image of the continuous globe,
opened an endless unknown; the sea becomes
infinity without definition. Midday sun
low across the water lightens its rhythmic edge,
the white break brilliant. Air cold and bright
contains the clarity of this place without parameters.

Home is stacking firewood, trimming herbs,
cutting back, burning invasive weed.
It is called keeping the place going.
A step away fog denies all security,
water has entered air, eliminated cliff,
earth, edges, all commonality.

# Cliffs of Fall

Below the high dark bluestone cliff
water is silver-plated between its boulders,
wattles hold gold up to the sky
and river redgums shine, their grey limbs
brighter than cloud, while shadows
of saplings lie across the creek
and wattlebirds go silly in the scrub.

Here in the shadow of the highway's bridge
you think of fertile dust – Rwanda, Sudan,
Palestine, Iraq and Lebanon, of reconciling difference,
of old massacres, stony rises and the great leaps.

# Second Thoughts

you had left my fantasy a month or so ago
and all was well and now I've let you in
again a silly thing to do

you must leave if you have not already
was it a curt farewell or did you feel
embarrassment keen on a hurried getaway

so much is contradictory – your new poem
I said too much about the dross of war
a hard poem – were you in Vietnam

were you recalling forty years ago
and you were thirty-something
still the pain persists like living flesh

you have come back – I dare not say a word
I said too much about imagined lives
and so you have returned

and I have let you in
please this is real haunting
and I am helpless now to hold the pain

# Portrait of a Poem

the substance of acronychal time
at the tip of night when a star rises
into coming dark a moment of sight
or caught before falling across an edge
of darkness into the light of day
that interval when words fall
beyond sound and sing

the fetch in the net of common tasks
shining fish in the curve of the web
that holds day together
the strange attractor
among the by-catch flesh that could
escape the order of necessity

the invisible point where two ways cross
without dimension the imagined point
where all roads meet and a word escapes
confinement direction definition
the place of death and possibility
the everyday footpath

the border between silence and dream
that demands translation to
quotidian speech a dance a channel
a watercourse you cannot live without
instead build dams to divert rivers
the hidden corner of a wish
the return of the bee to the hive

# Fantasy

Thinking I had lost the world and its pursuit;
a shadow image, tied to a repute, no way
to step outside that guarded field. You could,
but would not, cut closed boundaries,
release all expectations –
make me woman still.

I have sung poems, wonderful, tender and open,
shared my fragility, vulnerable, alone,
forgotten by the time I've found
pencil and paper.
The words are lost.

My need for you to hold, to be held, to say
something that is not wise. Words that will never live
in ink or graphite. The lost always the best.
When we next meet
will you speak to me?

Side by side talking of poetry, writing, joking
about winter wood, rubbish and bonfires
now forbidden, knowing I am, in years,
too old to expect much more
than familiar courtesy.

# In the Time

In the time when I want you
        to touch me without fear.
In the time when I imagine how it might be
        to be held without hesitation.
In the time when I know I must contain
        the silent wish.
In the time when I need to say, to write, I have
        partially known earth's heritage.

In this time I could mourn the past, but cannot
        wish for the impossible conjunction.
In this time who can say –
        this is all that matters?
In this time of age there is one answer
        in everybody's eyes.

# Traveller

'I will write,' you said. You will be far from writing, busy with people, places, the entry of all sound and shape, taste and touch of sun, rain, on the great stones of old towns. Stone that has soaked up time and action, blood and love, music and fear, the violence of competing tribes, the land of palaces and amber cells – how could you find time to write, and to whom? The friends, the friendship left behind, the need to shift all senses from living day, to days of regularity, the diary entries, the obligations. You will not write, and by the time you come again will have forgotten it was ever said, expected – the close touch of a hand.

# Tree Peony

A metre tall, branched and gnarled, dry buds
and scaly withered shoots from seasons failed:
a cutting I took from home, each winter promising
renewal, when shoots and buds make ready
for another year, their underground desire
to welcome mulching, leaves and deep sweet earth.

The cutting never flowered in my new land.
Soil too dry, too dark, too shallow. Shaded,
shadowed, in the only place open
and wide enough; stony ground perhaps.
Unwelcome, needing care, an old plant now.
Buds at every turn which fade and shrink.

*

Now after all these years the burst of flower:
a greening bud, a lengthening stem, escort of leaf.
Slowly the green globe swells, its helmet opens
in the morning sun. An intricate centre
cupped in unfurled wings, the blush of silk
that makes the damask rose seem plain and coarse.

Deep in its heart the ripening ring of gold,
the fivefold crimson grail of fertility sings
for an absent ghost. Years too late it has flowered
alone, opened old wounds. I think you might have
wished to be my lover at the cost of looking
for a gift, a power that I have lost.

# The Long Drought

The creek is turning to stone:
a tumbling of round
bleached basalt,
water-worn, vulnerable.

White sound trickles
through crowding boulders
in its starveling bed.

Silenced among dry rocks
the creek is losing its voice.

Catching light, twisting between stones
it plays a slow chorus
at the long rapids
before the bridge,

and falls silent
in the weed-clogged pool.

# Duck Business on Grey Goose Creek

I

In early spring the grey goose settles her own range:
the concrete foundation of the bridge across the creek,
the holding pool downstream before the rapids.
Queenly she sails the quiet water. Her bright
painted drake, another interloper from another land,
guards her explorations. He repels Teal, Black Duck
and Freckled, guards her territory, circles her,
attacks fleets of invaders. The creek ripples
with Trafalgars and Jutlands.

Early summer, fledgling time, he has gone, given up,
needing a smaller mate, a closer relative.
The grey goose keeps her territory alone.
On the island between the swimming reach
and the first rapid she squats in sedges.
But for the bright, fanned feet, the triangular orange bill,
she could be sun-bleached bluestone, just
one of the creek's boulders as its sluggish water
creeps into summer.

For years she has turned with seasons, forever lost,
unwelcome and alone. She keeps her native rounds,
the spring drake, false courtship, the tangled sedge,
summer and winter without company
watching from the foundations of the bridge.

Yesterday she was standing on a dark wet rock above
the reluctant stream, preening. Her white, beige,
dove-grey, buff, her fine short crest, all perfect
and beautiful among the sedge, the sludge, the summer algae,
the invasive weed. Her perfection shone in the black, still water;
she, immaculate, the solitary queen of a dreaming creek.

## II

Air still, a promise of morning sun, spring fever over.
Young duck breast the weed, feed, float, swim.
The white mallard heads a young flotilla
threading through the jungle. The lost grey goose
preens in thin dark water above the rapids.
The mallard leads mixed ducklings upstream
while the chestnut teals take their two
in tight formation away from the hoi polloi:
the pure black duck, and the mallard hybrids
with their give-away smudged eyebrows.

The next day, morning warm and quiet
between railway and overpass, the birds
foretaste summer survival on the shrinking creek.
The chestnut teal has kept his family close.
They dip and feed together in the shade. Gulls fly in,
retreat from attacking wings while balls of fluff
bounce and wobble and ride the rapids' waves.

The fleet of black have gone. Two, of the imperfect
eye-lining, dabble through the pool of weed:
the last pasturage in the shrinking creek.
The strange white drake hides his dull bronze head,
squats sunning on the footing of the bridge. Beside him,
a solitary basalt boulder shares the concrete slope:
the grey goose sleeping, in perfect balance on one orange leg.

# Time on the Merri Merri Creek

## Ninety Soon Enough

a calm time   release from all demand   only the day to face
like an infant year time expands and suddenly contracts
the year has gone   and days slow to a walking pace

there is no chance to control time letting go the poles
that keep days upright   days that might wash around the feet
surge and trip until the world is turning underfoot

running will not keep up   there's a high breaker coming
you might dive through or ride it to a safe landing
days when the slow opening of a lotus seems like eternity

measured in nanoseconds   a condensation of time and action
a mist across recognition   there is nothing to be done now
about the outcome of blood and love

# Time on the Merri Merri Creek

*Merri Merri* in the Wurundjeri language is 'stone stone' (many stones)

## I

There is afternoon, day's unreliable beauty,
the need to make the serpent friend; the traveller,
that other eye, asking help, from whom?
Help from absent gods, an imagined soul?
The cry is in the leaves and falling to the creek.
The creek is quiet, struggling, the drought-starved
water slow between its stones, dark and worn.
It must reach the river.

There is loss. The silent stranger's voice is saying *help*,
*help me*, to an unknown intangible,
a heart's heart, the only sightless sustenance.

On the footbridge, where slow rapids fall to a lower bed,
a black dog waits, avoids contact. His earth-brown mate
runs up, escorts the stranger over the bridge across the stream.

There is walking, each step follows another,
one foot further forward feels the path,
a motion through all bones, ligaments and skin.

There is loss – everyday's end left behind,
forgotten, and slow loss that inhabits quiet pools,
quick loss, perhaps a sudden fall, a long drop to the creek bed.
An old tributary preserved, channelled below the road,
covered by paths, roads and trains. In some seasons
it cascades across the basalt lip carried by the thrust
of change, seasons, growth and accident.

## II

There is the first loss when the future of the world
had no meaning, only the companionship of touch
and laughter, that lives and haunts. Sunset over the river
red-gold as a myth's treasure. All other mistakes,
misunderstandings, disappear, the first inevitable.
Almost everyone has lost in the first opening
of love's basket of tricks – there to be explored.

There is the second more vicious than the first.
For all women who have lost a child, known or not,
early or late, there is a time when the worldly wise
brush it off, 'Forget that one, go home and have another.'
And that lost and unknown child haunts all new beginnings;
fades until its next visit. It has made its point…

Friends fall away, they barely hurt or haunt, having shared
short stretches of lives, separated, remembered, they colour day.
Almost every action draws on the mind's well.

## III

The second haunts more sharply than the first,
although that first, buried less deeply, more pervasive,
easily returns, from other continents and another land.

There is one step after another, movement forward,
each uncertain foot momentarily aware of shape and slope.
In shadows by the stone stone creek a firebird in filtered sun
is only threads of sunlight on a weeping grass
leaning to the creek over water-sculpted stone.
A duck wings across the water.

There are those shaded ways of meeting loss.
They choose their haunting time together or alone.
After those two, none ever as homespun as before
but muddled in daily demands and the blowing wind.

## IV

There is the ocean's creek, the traveller has walked a path
through green shade and sun to meet the notice
propped by a heap of logs: 'Be careful Echidna lives here.'
Half beautiful, half serpent, she mothered monsters,
her name conferred on a survivor of centuries,
denizen of the shrinking creek with foxes, ducks,
eels, carp, and the water's heavy metals. She has lived
through the loss of everything but her need to live.

There are trees marked for destruction, willow, poplar, elm.
Felled, chipped, they will nurture sedge, wattle and gum
along the banks: an imagined memory, a deliberate renewal.
The creek will run to the river although its innocence is lost
and its fierce beginning, its tongue of lava, not within recall.

The chestnut teal lost all but one this spring.
Foxes live everywhere, hidden, silent, wise.
The birds behave as birds on a shrinking creek.
Teal, black duck, and a couple of cloudy hens, a hybrid drake,
a pair of foreign geese and a young darter
learning to swallow eels. An immigrant pigeon,
from some dry land, flies up into a dry drain
in the concave underbelly of the highway's bridge.

What if mind's ocean could withdraw from that harsh appeal,
feel in its resurgent tide more than the thought of loss:
the green growth of sedge, of leaves, of singing birds
along the struggling water of a starving creek?

# The Country of Nothing

In the country of nothing a long dry grows
quietly, slowly. You get used to it
and manage somehow: all desire slows
to the rhythm of silent days, you never admit

failure prolongs the drought, having done
all you can: fostered each hope of green,
nurtured all hint of swelling buds, but none
flourished and flowered into what might have been.

And then you came, falling like small rain
blown from a distance on a western wind.
Grain might have swelled and burgeoned once again
but the ground is dry and all the seeds are blind,

as when with time the body's functions cool
leaving the presence of an ageing fool.

# Duck Circles

Perfect circles surround each feeding bird
across the creek's rippling. Each bird breaks
bright suns in its wake, before its breast,
moving from hub to hub of the dipping rings.

The goose commands arcs from bank to bank,
the hybrid drake crosses her boundaries,
embroidered waves pattern the green shade.
A cyclist leans on the bridge's narrow rail,
throws down something saved from his packaged lunch.

A chase for the best chance. When the next piece falls
ducks congregate and flee, the goose turns on them all.
The creek's balance in chaos, its integrity fractured
by the casual intrusion of a new design.

# Mistake

The creek is black. Almost April waiting for autumn's change.
In the last long feeding pool black duck and the hybrid mallard
    circle each other.
    The teal sleep
on dry basalt rocks between stones bound to hold curling rapids
    when rain arrives.
    Under the overhead bridge the solitary goose
    circles in brilliant white, dove-grey and scarlet bill.
I have called that goose solitary, lost, barely welcome in a foreign land
    and now it is
    circling, circling
    a fine grey goose,
an elegant, slim, grey goose of the curving neck, without a crest,
lacking a scarlet bill. She is tangerine-billed and the bird
I have watched for years, amazed at the purity of feather,
    the colour, the fine crest,
    no longer the isolated Artemis of the creek, a danger
    to all who see,
    is Odysseus or Achilles.
He circles the goose of the snake-like neck and gentle grey.
    They feed
    side by side,
    back to back,
    facing each other.
I wonder whether they will nest among the rubbish and weeds
    along the creek below the bridge.

Without a gaggle
as defence against the fox,
will the creek splash, rustle and sing to small grey bits of fluff
after September?
Should I pray
that the great grey goosey gander will not wander from his
improbable mate?
Later the creek's carers say
she arrived at midnight
in a cardboard box.

# After Drought a Day of Wind

The wind had changed.
A north-easterly, humid
with tropical unease,
faded before the desert's
onslaught that disturbed
all sense, then it shifted round.

Walking home, breathing
the ocean of cool relief
under footpath trees starving
into a new season, instantly
aware of easy ridicule,
I breathed-in a choking fly.

I could not leave it scratching
somewhere in a sea of spit
and unswallowable tongue,
eventually rescued it in a tide
of all that stuff you spit out at the dentist's.

A tiny thing, golden-brown and round,
a ringed Saturn: a winged seed.
Then I should have turned back
to the last two trees to find
which tree, what wind, had blown its future
into my open mouth.

# Reply

And you have replied. I did not expect to hear
after my tangential acknowledgement
of those years before. A time for clean surgery;
for two ways to diverge into the separate
pains of other years.

And you have replied. Did you miss
the tense division between counting backwards
or forwards anyone could see?
wonder how the gulf of years
could be crossed backwards?

It's easy to follow heart first. But the moon's water,
time that she can never turn back, even to meet
gracefully the embrace of a new tributary,
recedes quickly at the end of the ebb.
These poems are all too old.

# The Colour of Water

Watching the great grey sea
thinking only of light,
swift facets, wind ripple,
the colour of moving water.

The only time I stop thinking
of you. Remembering
movement, voice
subtle as the sea.

# Welcome to This Space

That I have lived in, almost
approaching you.

An empty plain, changeless
for a long while now shifts

continually, edges move and slide,
look different from where you stand

or walk or sleep, the only stable
place, the shape it now is

and one day will be different.
I leave all this space

for you with my own stain on,
around, within, knowing it is yours.

# Sudden Rain

Sapling-sheltered by elm and poplar-suckered scrub,
cut and mulched onto the embankment, the river red
lost its top when the wind came with an abundant load.
One branch, held out to sluice the rain more gently to the ground,
holds the young tree's imperfect balance on the slope
up to the railway line above the creek. The ringtail nest
hangs, still secure, in the young wattle's grasp.
Runnel tracks cross roots, banks, paths, driven leaves.

The creek grew fat and fierce on Sunday night, swept
the flood plain, held to attention by its basalt walls.
Flattened sedges face downstream. A black duck
leads its young bouncing down rapids before the bridge,
pulls into the sheltering bank to pause and feed.

A confusion of broken branches, dead wood, fallen debris,
lie across the footbridge, up the banks, carried like a wave
to weave wild tangles against the trees. The rain on Sunday night
filled the watercourse, threw all the failures of a dry year,
all unaccountable wishes, into full view from the public railway line.

# The Creek's Summer

The creek has fallen below the rapids' alto, the stones' bass.
Sedges wear their summer biscuit-gold and white.

Anxious black duck head upstream towards the bridge
and a pair of elegant, iridescent chestnut teal
turn their backs on the silent weed-logged pool.

A darter fishes along the mud-cliff bank, broken
and crumbling below its load of weed. The two geese
sail, grandly in line ahead, from the upper reach
to review the remains of all their winter fleet.

Silence is heavy in the summer air,
dulled senses fade, withdraw from all congress
with traffic of the mind, the heart shrinks
and resounds only to the rhythm of heat and loss.

# The Edge of Winter

## Having a Good Day

It's when you pick up the pen

                              find paper before sitting down

It's then you go out to buy

                              something you do not need

in order to talk to someone

                              you do not know

about the weather outside the shop

                              the night was cold

the rain has stopped

                              while you fumble having no fives or tens

only a fifty   then a handful of coin and paper.

                              *Have a good day.*

# All the Paths Are Dry

Hazy night has provided enough fog for sedge and grass
to bow under drops; enough to give the creek a quiet
voice, and power to sweep away livid, yellow, willow leaves.

Water refreshed – with some hurry – is sweeping a clean channel.
Water that does not break and sing between stones
rejects the light. Below poplars, a silvering carpet,

grey, white and black, 'No colour,' the photographer said –
a mosaic of dead leaves, black and white and grey.
Water, darker than leaves, breaks brilliant across stone.

I cannot write words the creek has given. Having to do,
to see, say this or that, the words I bring back rearrange
themselves, no longer speak of the coldly quiet morning by the creek.

Usually it offers words of process, care and neglect, of all
complexities, but now disorder drowns its voice, leaves lost words,
crooked sentences – none saying tomorrow or perhaps.

# The End of Winter

In the half-and-half time when winter fades before inevitable change
I walk between the old volcano's print and the railway to the city's
negative. Between its basalt cliffs, sun and wind drive the creek's
wattle-thick air through sedges, trees, the path to the river.

Stone and water mix, a mercurial stream, rough going
for spring's new hatchlings. They wobble, bounce and falter. The seagull
has returned to his patch under the highway bridge.
His hunting ground for the year's first ducklings.

Rain and sudden sun together join the burdened air. Wattles
pour their brilliance across the flow. Only a few weeks now
to official spring, but water and the creek's trees know, and the seagulls
have come back to where time lies, and builds, and kills.

The gull picks at rocks where small fish face the current
small as a seagull's beak, dark as the basalt bed. Wattles
spread incense heavy as thought through saturated light indifferent
to whatever drought or abundance the darkening spring will bring.

# Continuance

In cold air I look at the grey sea shining
see the colour of light   touch
the beauty of fallen sea-sculpted trees

touch the edge   see a continuance
driving towards what I cannot tell

Death so often looks like life

# Transition

An ageing frame's not built to fall in love,
rebuild desire, rehearse the pains of youth
on a neglected stage; slowly uncover
plays masked by the face of social truth.
The wrinkled skin, thin hair, a wobbly gait
are not enough to undermine the power
of magnetism, although it seems too late
for such attraction to break bounds and flower.

The air is charged. Plain time throbs and spins
where every meeting lifts a scaffolding
to raise the wider bridge where trust begins,
and every parting's doubts left lingering.

The mind's blood tastes, with every living breath,
whether one will be mourning the other's death.

# The Portuguese Fish Basket

Surprised to meet an intriguing light
in woven whitewood: fine strapping like corded silk,
half boat, half sideways egg, I bought it
in an avant-garde, upfront, high-tone boutique:
an impulse to engage with its beauty,
its total practicality.

It carried fish for the family from the market,
heads resting against the woven wood,
eyes smiling and comfortable. It held to
the deep sun-splashed windowsill
like a throne, like a ritual boat. Straked sides, a curving base
bound to a wattled rim, the whole shell woven as one
to strong gunwales with sleaved wood like bands of silk,
held fruit for the children: apples, bananas,
and one small bowl for small unthought-of things.

In another hemisphere, it played a role as crib
for a small saviour, tried out for parts in school plays –
unsuitable for poisoned apples, the director said.
It could hold a pumpkin on its side,
until fetched on command, without capsizing.

After the children left, it lived on above the sink
cradling ginger and garlic and a few strange fruit:
avocado, custard apple, purple figs. In time
it collected dust. A hulk, it lost
its half-shining creamy glow, its silky touch,
held corks and candle-ends in the small bowl,
garlic and ginger, until it had to move.

Still holding the air of continents and the strength
of trees, it moved to a narrow room,
still remembering fish, and the hands that wove
forest into a coracle. Dirty and dull,
washed with care, scrubbed a little, dust
rinsed away, its weft and woof exchanging light,
the silky woven flesh shone again – satin.
An old vessel, ready for fish, fruit, or dreams,
whatever you need to take into the next room.

Propped against a geranium, the basket dripped water
in the return corner of a ramp linking cottages:
a ramp that allowed the frail and weak to walk
to ground level – look, no steps – a rail, a web of wire,
a corner to hold the geranium.

The potted flower, steel wire, careful ramp,
shrunk rooms, all intimations of time
that has passed and memory. A frail evening wind
blew into the basket's hull. The Portuguese
fish basket fell across the boards, open, vulnerable.

And kicked. It would not slide below the wires,
would not fly, bounced back from a kicking foot,
kicked and kicked and kicked. It lay sideways,
half-strangled by the wire below my window
above the ramp, the wire and the red geranium.
I brought the basket in. My neighbour of the ramp
has not seen me. She has stopped kicking, retired.
We share the ramp. We need to reach the ground.

Now the basket lies in the shelter of a fridge,
holds a knob of ginger, garlic and tomatoes
still remembering the fish it used to hold, smiling,
coming from the bustling market in the square,
and forests of woven light in another continent.

# Holiday

A few precious days – away, a holiday –
from the place called mine
borrowed for an unknown time
where one learns the ropes
and isolation shrinks to nothing
until days become a road without
a lane to return on
where everybody 'fits' the category –
alone, aged, loath to say
'I am at home' until
that harlequin mediator time
stops his dance in space.

# Pool

Imagine – no, think – a leafless winter tree
above a still pool. The sun gentle, watch
reflections in the pool, and a Little Grebe
dressed for breeding near the tree's mirror.
It dips and bobs, makes sure every feather sits
and around it perfect circles spread. Dark and light
cross the perfect image of the tree and break the pattern
of silence with satellite rings of action.

Analysis and solution might be possible if you had
perfect photography, a computer with eyes
for oblique measurements: that pattern could be
sampled in nanoseconds, and explained. There must be
maths for it, if you had the means. I watch the reflection
of a tree, a small bird preening, and the whole world
change – patterns I live with and barely understand:
a Little Grebe in breeding colours, alone, preening
in an old volcano's silent, accidental pool.

# The Table

I look at you across the table and see smooth skin, the delicate mouth, and see how you are young. I look across the table and see how carefully you dressed. I look at you, the sun behind me, on my back. I see you in semi-shadow and wish the sun to stop in his track, the world to stop in its orbit, the moment to fall across the table like a shadow, impregnate the wood. The shadow will cross the table. I will remember this day. The table between us, as real as the sun behind my back, has suffered the many faces of shade and light. The shadow across your face. The grain of wood, quiet grey, weathered by sun and storm. It feels like suede, has held memories, all of them forgotten.

# The Dark Side of the Eclipse

## No Longer

I could wait no longer having tried
every avoidance possible for so long:
a time of patience and friendship
helping each other, a line, a reference,
minor irritations, discoveries and stories:
a time of patience and waiting until
that day of desperation. Mind and body
and the day no longer articulate.
When I rang you, I could barely speak.

Sunshine and champagne on the table, always
champagne for the current issue, the currency
of amity on the table, a laugh, a careless
leaning back, the deep well of daily trust
opening, leaning back, laughing: *I have a partner*.

# Edge

I thought to loose him in the ocean; in the ocean
that he rode under starlight, under moonlight under storm.
In cold breakers I would lose him, in the breakers
I could swim through, I could ride.

In moving water there is no one, only water,
moving water, you are one among the creatures of the ocean,
all the wild unknowing creatures of the ocean –
of the fringe of ocean, and the power of the sea.

Late this day the sea was strong, retreating to the moon,
after its highest reach, under the hottest day.
The north wind blew against its rise, flattened
its wildest peaks until the edge of change

swept through the hills, stormed across the water.
Wind and tide again opposed, more fiercely than before.
Moon-time ebb had come to pull the ocean back,
and sudden turncoat wind drove it towards the shore.

I swam against the wind, feeling the tide
almost beyond the impulse to return
to land, firm land, the dry, dark bed of clay
and sand and rock, shoreline's confining edge,
the limits of desire.

I turned and rode a shallow breaker in, its crest
rushing to land until it died in foam,
left me in shallow water pulling, pulling back.
There I could not stand against the tide,
feet in slipping sand, the wind driving onwards,
the water pulling, pulling. There I crawled –
a turtle, wanting paddles, wanting shell –
fell forward, staggering in the sand

to stand against the wind, and turned to face
the old moon's ocean's power: the driven crests,
the sucking curl above the pulsing deep,
the dark cold undertow, the surface toss,

water, foam and spray driving above
the silent stillness of the moon's own element;
and faced the wind, without a thought of loss,
welcomed the sea, the sea that ebbed and flowed,

the air that drove the cutting sand, the flying spray –
confluence of air and sea and land, and yet
content, after that raging turmoil
no one could forget.

# Return

I did not expect to be disturbed so much
when I withdrew, then felt relief and calm;
no longer dodging words, avoiding touch,
      secure from harm,
and still near falling for that easy charm,
careful to keep to ordinary things.

But you've returned again – your message come
proposing the need to meet – return some books,
to clear, perhaps, something misunderstood.
      And I will come.
My peace has gone, disrupted by the hooks
within that web of words that leaves me numb

and defenceless. You have said nothing wrong.
Though my consent to meet has been polite,
this friendship, of a kind, has been too long
      to quarrel now,
too close, too dear, which might have bred delight;
so let's thank time for all it will allow.

# Inside Out

'I love long life better than figs.' (*Antony and Cleopatra*)

Once it was said the apple caused all the trouble,
but the climate's wrong, the land of hubble-bubble
and lots of ease and time, no need for sex.
Let's find an alternative that does not so perplex.
There's a strong candidate: the pomegranate,
tough and resistant. I'd not bet my trousers on it.

It could be the glorious, golden, perfumed quince:
the climate's better but opinion's altered since
it was declared inedible without a lot of cooking.
So let's consider how to find another: looking
up old texts, using imagination – there's the apricot.
It's in the poem of poems, but it is not

firm enough to last a day of heat. For something not too big
but strong and secret, plump and delectable, let's try the fig.
It's inside out. The wasps have lots of fun and clown about,
and enter, and they're caught inside and upside down.
Helpless, they're not worth a fig. But believe just what you please.
Forget Cleo and Tony, Act I scene 2 – just enjoy your cheese.

# Fig Reply

I'll fear no evil in the grave's embrace,
that silent, private place;
Marvell understood the peak of all endeavour
and wrote a poem that will last forever.
Keep to the grape. It's pretty and refined
and washes all the nonsense from the mind.

# The House I Have Left Behind

The garden I left in autumn, tidied up
for new people, is a riot of purple, gold and green
among winter's neighbours, drab since the dry.
It has shouted another spring and its hard rain.
The long drought died after the second winter
and the garden knew long before anyone
that its time had come. Rosemary's falling arcs,
purple-blue for the sun's light and wallflowers, gold –
russet-stained to remember its species genes.

The tubbed lime on the veranda died a year ago;
the shrivelled border of box below its lip
greening at last. Winter iris struggle through tangles
of uncut leaf, their blue and gold carried into the earth,
and neglected lavenders thrust dry, infertile brush
through the shining flood. The rose, the Mermaid,
stands ragged; withered flowers among sprouting leaves.

The garden I gave to someone else: my face to the road,
the neighbourhood, the world, all I could leave them,
unvalued in the price, left to itself and the seasons: like
the broken bones of a geranium warped to the iron fence.
The passer-by will see only the riot of gold and purple,
smell the unavoidable fragrance of flowers, self-sown,
perennial, from the stone walls of another country,
and the bee-haunted arcs of purple flowering:
the persistence of roots that will not be forgotten.

# Still Life – A Portrait

I wonder whether age is worthless when
the problems youth endures and survives
recur after years of drought: an aching drought
of laughter, warmth and joy
breaks in a tide of energy.
Its flood frees an elusive pain,
an impetus that secretly
becomes a daily charge.

Day's light and night's dark pause,
as when painters catch and hold
all seasons in one hour; everything
sealed behind translucent glaze.

And when the image falters before the eye
a changeling spell strips off the surface gloss,
conjures fantasy, mirage, parody,
hidden shadows wait behind its face.

There's no way back or forward, but to turn,
face empty air, the trace of a voice,
a trusted hand, friendship's bond.

Still life ensures that day and night,
all earth's elements and all earth's pain,
ageing alone can gather into one
behind its unseen, unknown silences.

# The Large Hadron Collider

What Can the Matter Be?

Once again that inevitable conflict shouts
through keyholes, from telephones, in emails,
across the table, 'Who are you and why?'
constantly defined between the grasp of pliers
in an unknown hand, and the beauty of an art
that continually sheds its face to show
another view. In an intangible moment when
an electric energy and gravity collide

what can the matter be? and why and where
did it survive? Words fall short of what can not
be seen or felt, only life's leftovers: only love
and living, neither explicable. We try to limn
shadows' substance, the old wisdom and the new,
our legend inadequate and always out of tune.

# There is a Time of Day

There is a time of day,
all possible tasks complete,
some, perhaps, left for another time,
when I think of what is neither seen nor heard:
the sound of a voice no longer near.

Distant images return, fade and move,
and then there is only night until
another morning opens another set
of tasks and duties, all activity
designed to fill the hours before
that creeping silence calls
and calls from where I cannot see,
dare not imagine – there where you are.

# The Dark Side of the Eclipse

During the eclipse I saw, long ago, the moon
so wonderfully red, almost translucent.
In harmony, all the birds stopped singing, waited

for its dark, that other dark, the bottom of a dream,
so deep I cannot tell its features – what it might carry,
what its other side is like.

Darker than dark, beyond thought.
The dark's own light is there somewhere,
inextinguishable, indestructible.

# The Poem I Will Forget

It is there, or was: grew in a new spring
under earth spread across a sandstone bed
on a lonely continent, climbed through
the distances and tangles of a beginning.

After dark and cold, drought and freezing sleet
it came into a sun and the southern ocean's
air and a fresh uncontaminated flood
from unknown reaches of enticement

and continuance. The poem spread a little,
acknowledged other airs and times, tasted
influences from the whole world
to be seen, rejected, used, noticed or ignored.

It made little noise, unlike invisible wind
in tall trees, the beating of the ocean
on the shore, like the distances of moon
and sun and stars and all the galaxies.

It was only a small poem, neither beautiful nor
brilliant like the stars or the voluptuous lotus.

Look, there it is, written down at last. Like all that's
faded, no longer a part in the confrontations of time
and survival, it left nothing behind, took very little
away, only the breath of the great ocean and the sun.

## The Creek in Winter

(2012)

Still the same, worn stones and water's rapids
have words this day, sunlight on broken water;
the creek meets bluestone aware of the current.

Dark basalt built in fire in this low sun is bright
as the broken water, polished by light.
The dull brown creek flings itself
between sun and rock and catches fire.

*The Edge of Winter* is Connie Barber's fifth collection of poetry since her poems began to be published in the mid-1970s in literary journals in Australia and overseas. She was born in Sydney in 1922, studied art at the Melbourne Technical College (1939–42), served in the AWAS (1942–46), and graduated from the University of Melbourne in 1951 with an honours BA in English. After periods of residence in England during the 1950s and '60s, she taught in Victorian secondary schools (1971–82), painted and exhibited in Melbourne, and taught creative writing at the CAE and in community writing groups.

www.ingramcontent.com/pod-product-compliance
Lightning Source LLC
Chambersburg PA
CBHW062149100526
44589CB00014B/1749